REDD+ and Business Sustainability

A Guide to Reversing Deforestation for Forward Thinking Companies

Brian Joseph McFarland

Carbonfund.org Foundation, Inc.

Brian.McFarland@Carbonfund.org

First published in 2013 by Dō Sustainability

87 Lonsdale Road, Oxford OX2 7ET, UK

ISBN 978-1-909293-34-2 (eBook-ePub)
ISBN 978-1-909293-35-9 (eBook-PDF)
ISBN 978-1-909293-33-5 (Paperback)

A catalogue record for this title is available from the British Library.

Dō Sustainability strives for net positive social and environmental impact. See our sustainability policy at **www.dosustainability.com**.

Page design and typesetting by Alison Rayner
Cover by Becky Chilcott

For further information on Dō Sustainability, visit our website:
www.dosustainability.com

DōShorts

Dō Sustainability is the publisher of **DōShorts**: short, high-value ebooks that distil sustainability best practice and business insights for busy, results-driven professionals. Each DōShort can be read in 90 minutes.

New and forthcoming DōShorts – stay up to date

We publish 3 to 5 new DōShorts each month. The best way to keep up to date? Sign up to our short, monthly newsletter. Go to **www. dosustainability.com/newsletter** to sign up to the Dō Newsletter. Some of our latest and forthcoming titles include:

- *Green Jujitsu: Embed Sustainability into Your Organisation* Gareth Kane

- *How to Make your Company a Recognised Sustainability Champion* Brendan May

- *Making the Most of Standards* Adrian Henriques

- *Promoting Sustainable Behaviour: A Practical Guide to What Works* Adam Corner

- *How to Account for Sustainability* Laura Musikanski

- *Sustainability in the Public Sector* Sonja Powell

- *Sustainability Reporting for SMEs* Elaine Cohen

- *Sustainable Transport Fuels Business Briefing* David Thorpe

- *The Changing Profile of Corporate Climate Change Risk* Mark Trexler & Laura Kosloff

- *The First 100 Days: Plan, Prioritise & Build a Sustainable Organisation* Anne Augustine

- *The Short Guide to SRI* Cary Krosinsky

Subscriptions

In additional to individual sales and rentals, we offer individual and organisational subscriptions to our full collection of published and forthcoming books. To discuss a subscription for yourself or your organisation, email **veruschka@dosustainability.com**

Write for us, or suggest a DōShort

Please visit **www.dosustainability.com** for our full publishing programme. If you don't find what you need, write for us! Or suggest a DōShort on our website. We look forward to hearing from you.

....

Abstract

HOW CAN FORWARD-THINKING sustainability leaders reverse tropical deforestation? What exactly are payment for ecosystem service forest conservation projects, otherwise known as Reducing Emissions from Deforestation and Degradation (REDD+), and how can these projects contribute to business sustainability and profitability? Why are deforestation and degradation important and how are leading companies making a positive impact on tropical forest conservation and mitigating greenhouse gas emissions through direct support of REDD+ projects? Such topics are extremely important because tropical forests are quickly disappearing – at a rate of nearly one football or soccer field every few seconds – while REDD+ simultaneously offers a scalable conservation finance mechanism and a platform for business sustainability. This DōShort on REDD+ is a practical publication targeted to busy business professionals and focuses on the nexus between tropical forest conservation projects and the sustainability practices of major global businesses. The book begins by contextualizing the issues at hand through identifying the location of the world's remaining forests, exploring where and why deforestation and degradation is occurring, and then briefly explaining the importance of mitigating deforestation and preserving ecosystem services, which are essentially the goods and services provided for free by nature. After this context setting, the book defines REDD+ and focuses on its significance to business sustainability including, but not limited to, the role of REDD+ in: mitigating global greenhouse gas emissions while reducing business risk to a changing

ABSTRACT

climate; as part of a firm's philanthropic work; as a mechanism to increase consumer loyalty; benefitting upstream local communities and ecosystem services; enhancing corporate social responsibility image and upholding corporate principles; and providing unique marketing opportunities and product positioning through private sector support of charismatic REDD+ projects. Next, a detailed look at REDD+ business case studies and best practices will be presented. This includes how to: develop your own REDD+ project; donate to a nonprofit organization that is supporting REDD+ projects; invest in a company that is developing REDD+ projects; invest directly into a particular REDD+ project; or invest into a pooled fund. The final section highlights the future of REDD+, which provides a promising mechanism for financing forest conservation while increasing the sustainability and profitability of forward-thinking sustainable leaders. The potential future demand and supply of REDD+ projects, along with future financing arrangements, is explored.

About the Author

 **BRIAN McFARLAND** is currently the Portfolio Manager at Carbonfund.org Foundation, Inc. and the Project Origination Manager at CarbonCo LLC, the wholly owned subsidiary of Carbonfund.org.

At Carbonfund.org, he identifies climate change mitigation projects in the energy efficiency, renewable energy, and forestry sectors, conducts due diligence on such projects, and then structures the financial support and manages the project portfolio. This multi-million dollar project portfolio includes approximately 75 tree planting and carbon reduction projects across more than 30 US states and more than 15 countries. At CarbonCo, he identifies early stage forest conservation projects and then designs and implements the origination of Reducing Emissions from Deforestation and Degradation (REDD+) projects. This includes spearheading the first ever dual Verified Carbon Standard and Climate, Community and Biodiversity Standard validated REDD+ project in the State of Acre, Brazil. Brian McFarland is a CSA Standards Certified GHG Inventory Quantifier and a member of the Metropolitan Washington Council of Governments' Air and Climate Public Advisory Committee. He earned a dual graduate degree in Business Administration and Global Environmental Policy from American University, where his thesis was entitled 'Origins, Development and Potential of the International REDD Market.'

The opinions expressed in this DōShort are those of the author and do not necessarily represent the views of Carbonfund.org or CarbonCo.

Acknowledgments

THE AUTHOR WOULD LIKE TO THANK his friends and family for their support, along with a particular thank you to Gabriel Thoumi who provided numerous rounds of comments and thoughtful insights to strengthen this DōShort on REDD+. In addition, the author would like to acknowledge the forward-thinking companies, local communities, and dedicated professionals working around the clock to reverse tropical deforestation.

Acronyms and Definitions

ACR American Carbon Registry – The ACR is a leading certification standard for the voluntary carbon markets.

CAR Climate Action Reserve – The CAR is a leading certification standard for the voluntary carbon markets.

CCBA/CCBS Climate, Community and Biodiversity Alliance/Climate, Community and Biodiversity Standard – The CCBA created the CCBS; the CCBS is a design standard for carbon projects to demonstrate net positive biodiversity and community benefits.

CO_2e Carbon Dioxide Equivalent Emissions – CO_2e is a unit of measure to equate the global warming potential of the different greenhouse gas emissions.

CSR Corporate Social Responsibility – CSR is the various actions undertaken by corporate actors to positively benefit stakeholders.

FAO United Nations' Food and Agricultural Organization – FAO is the United Nations organization specializing in global food and agricultural activities.

GHG Greenhouse Gasses – GHGs are the gas emissions which contribute to global climate change. The six greenhouse gases, as regulated by the Kyoto Protocol, are carbon dioxide, methane, nitrous oxides, sulfur hexafluoride, perfluorocarbons, and hydrofluorocarbons.

REDD/REDD+ Reducing Emissions from Deforestation and Degradation/ REDD+ – According to the United Nations REDD Programme, REDD is described as 'an effort to create a financial value for the carbon stored in forests, offering incentives for developing countries to reduce emissions from forested lands and invest in low-carbon paths to sustainable development'.[1] The '+' designates REDD and the additional activities of forest conservation, sustainable forest management, and the enhancement of carbon stocks.

OECD Organization for Economic Co-operation and Development – The OECD is a government forum that works on economic, social, and environmental issues.

PDs/PDDs Project Documents/Project Design Documents – PDs/PDDs are the documents required for a carbon project to be validated and verified to a given certification standard.

PES Payment for Ecosystem Services – PES are the financial benefits paid for the collective goods and services provided by nature.

RFPs Request for Proposals – RFPs are guidance documents outlining the requirements and timelines for a service provider to incorporate in their proposal.

UNFCCC United Nations Framework Convention on Climate Change – The UNFCCC is the international treaty tasked with addressing global climate change.

VCS Verified Carbon Standard – The VCS is a leading certification standard for the voluntary carbon markets.

VERs Verified Emission Reductions – VERs are the equivalent of one metric tonne of CO_2e that has been mitigated or sequestered. VERs are also known as carbon credits.

To review the official US Government finance and carbon markets lexicon used by the US Agency for International Development's Forest Carbon, Markets and Communities program, see here for English (**http://www.fcmcglobal. org/documents/FinanceandCarbonMarketsLexiconFinal40clean.pdf**) and here for Spanish (**http://www.fcmcglobal.org/documents/Carbonolexico-Spanish%20V1-0.pdf**).

Contents

CHAPTER 1

The World's Forests and Global Deforestation and Degradation

WHERE ARE THE WORLD'S REMAINING FORESTS LOCATED? Are deforestation and degradation major environmental issues? If so, where are such deforestation and degradation occurring and what are their main drivers?

Forest cover

Table 1 depicts the top 20 countries with the largest total forest area according to the State of the World's Forests 2011 Report issued by the United Nations' Food and Agricultural Organization (FAO).

TABLE 1. Top 20 forested countries as of 2010: Extent of forest area[2] (FAO data)

	Country	2010 Forest area (hectares)	2010 Forest area (acres)
1	Russian Federation	809,090,000	1,998,452,300
2	Brazil	519,522,000	1,283,219,340
3	Canada	310,134,000	766,030,980
4	USA	304,022,000	750,934,340
5	China	206,861,000	510,946,670

6	Dem. Republic of Congo	154,135,000	380,713,450
7	Australia	149,300,000	368,771,000
8	Indonesia	94,432,000	233,247,040
9	Sudan	69,949,000	172,774,030
10	India	68,434,000	169,031,980
11	Peru	67,992,000	167,940,240
12	Mexico	64,802,000	160,060,940
13	Colombia	60,499,000	149,432,530
14	Angola	58,480,000	144,445,600
15	Bolivia	57,196,000	141,274,120
16	Zambia	49,468,000	122,185,960
17	Venezuela	46,275,000	114,299,250
18	Mozambique	39,022,000	96,384,340
19	Tanzania	33,428,000	82,567,160
20	Myanmar	31,773,000	78,479,310

From this we can see that among the top forested countries, those with the greatest total forest area tend to be the countries with the largest overall land mass. Thus, the top five countries in terms of land mass are:

- #1: Russia (#1 in total forest area)
- #2: Canada (#3 in total forest area)
- #3: China (#5 in total forest area)
- #4 USA (#4 in total forest area)
- #5 Brazil (#2 in total forest area)[3]

....

MAP 1. Top 20 forested countries by hectares in 2010 (FAO data)[4]

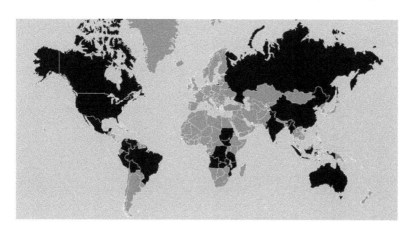

....

While there were still approximately 4.03 billion hectares (9.95 billion acres or 15.57 million square miles) of forests remaining as of 2011, deforestation and degradation are especially severe in select regions. Here this is leading to fragmented, degraded landscapes with declining ecosystem services, contributing to global climate change through the release of greenhouse gas emissions.[2]

Deforestation and degradation

In general, cattle-ranching is the main reason for deforestation and degradation in Central and South America. In Southeast Asia timber and palm oil production are the main causes, while in sub-Saharan Africa fuelwood collection and subsistence agriculture are the primary drivers. Globally, commercial agriculture – particularly of soy beans – is also a major factor.

The Nature Conservancy states that only 2% of the world's total surface area is covered in rainforests, yet 'every second, a slice of rainforest the size of a football field is mowed down. That's 86,400 football fields of rainforest per day, or over 31 million football fields of rainforest each year.'[5]

Similarly according to Dr. William Laurance of the Smithsonian Tropical Research Institute, the rate of deforestation of the Amazon rainforest during the mid-1990s was 3.5 million acres (i.e. 1.42 million hectares) a year; between 2003 and 2005, this rate was closer to 6.5 million acres (2.63 million hectares) each year. This is the equivalent of seven to ten football fields deforested every minute for three successive years.[6]

Tables 2 and 3 show the highest net loss of forests from the periods 1990–2000 and 2000–2010, according to the State of the World's Forests 2011 Report issued by the United Nations' FAO.

TABLE 2. Top 20 forest cover annual change rates: 1990–2000 (hectares and acres)[2] (FAO data)

	Country	Annual change rate 1990–2000 (hectares)	Annual change rate 1990–2000 (acres)
1	Brazil	-2,890,000	-7,138,300
2	Indonesia	-1,914,000	-4,727,580
3	Sudan	-589,000	-1,454,830
4	Myanmar	-435,000	-1,074,450
5	Nigeria	-410,000	-1,012,700
6	Tanzania	-403,000	-995,410
7	Mexico	-354,000	-874,380
8	Zimbabwe	-327,000	-807,690
9	Dem. Republic of Congo	-311,000	-768,170
10	Argentina	-293,000	-723,710
11	Venezuela	-288,000	-711,360
12	Bolivia	-270,000	-666,900
13	Cameroon	-220,000	-543,400
14	Mozambique	-219,000	-540,930
15	Ecuador	-198,000	-489,060
16	Paraguay	-179,000	-442,130
17	Honduras	-174,000	-429,780
18	Zambia	-167,000	-412,490
19	Ethiopia	-141,000	-348,270
20	Cambodia	-140,000	-345,800

TABLE 3. Top 20 forest cover annual change rates: 2000–2010 (hectares and acres)[2] (FAO data)

	Country	Annual change rate 2000–2010 (hectares)	Annual change rate 2000–2010 (acres)
1	Brazil	-2,642,000	-6,525,740
2	Australia	-562,000	-1,388,140
3	Indonesia	-498,000	-1,230,060
4	Nigeria	-410,000	-1,012,700
5	Tanzania	-403,000	-995,410
6	Zimbabwe	-327,000	-807,690
7	Dem. Republic of Congo	-311,000	-768,170
8	Myanmar	-310,000	-765,700
9	Bolivia	-290,000	-716,300
10	Venezuela	-288,000	-711,360
11	Argentina	-246,000	-607,620
12	Cameroon	-220,000	-543,400
13	Mozambique	-217,000	-535,990
14	Ecuador	-198,000	-489,060
15	Mexico	-195,000	-481,650
16	Paraguay	-179,000	-442,130
17	Zambia	-167,000	-412,490
18	Cambodia	-145,000	-358,150
T20	Ethiopia	-141,000	-348,270
T20	Papua New Guinea	-141,000	-348,270

MAP 2. Top 20 most deforested countries by net change in hectares, 2000–2010 (FAO data)[4]

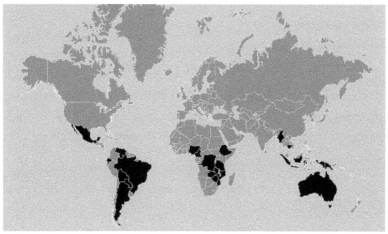

It is clear that South American and sub-Saharan African countries are highly represented in the historical deforestation trends of 1990–2000 and 2000–2010. For example, five of the top ten in terms of net loss of hectares (Sudan, Nigeria, Tanzania, Zimbabwe, and the Democratic Republic of Congo) in 1990–2000 and four of the top ten in net loss of hectares (Nigeria, Tanzania, Zimbabwe, and the Democratic Republic of Congo) in 2000–2010 were sub-Saharan African countries.

It is important to note that Brazil, Australia, and Indonesia collectively had more land cleared than the remaining nations ranked fourth to sixteenth for 2000–2010. In addition, only two Organization for Economic Co-operation and Development (OECD) countries were listed in the top 20: Australia and Mexico[7] with an average of 562,000 hectares (1,388,140 acres) and 195,000 hectares (481,650 acres) cleared each year during 2000–2010, respectively. Yet it is also important to recognize that such OECD countries are frequently the end users of global commodities: in 2004 they consumed approximately 86% of the world's aluminum, 81% of the world's paper, 80% of the world's iron and steel, 76% of the world's timber, and owned 87% of the world's vehicles.[8]

Furthermore, after reviewing those countries with the highest levels of deforestation, the vast majority may be considered to have corrupt governance, to be experiencing a conflict, to be located in the Southern Hemisphere or along the equator, and/or to have weak institutions.

For example, comparing the 2000–2010 listed countries to Transparency International's Corruption Perceptions Index 2011, Myanmar was ranked 180th out of the world's 182 most corrupt countries, Venezuela was in joint 172nd position, the Democratic Republic of Congo was 168th, Cambodia 164th, and Zimbabwe 154th.[9]

Similarly, according to the Brookings Institution and the World Bank Group's Worldwide Governance Indicators Project covering 215 economies over the 1996–2011 time period, Myanmar was the sixth lowest rated country on the Voice and Accountability indicator; the Democratic Republic of Congo tied for fifth lowest on Political Stability and Absence of Violence; Myanmar and the Democratic Republic of Congo were joint fifth lowest on Government Effectiveness; Zimbabwe was tied for fifth lowest on Regulatory Quality; Zimbabwe and Venezuela were tied for third lowest on Rule of Law; and Myanmar was the lowest rated on the Control of Corruption indicator.[10]

In addition, Nigeria, the Democratic Republic of Congo, Myanmar, and Mexico are all currently experiencing, or relatively recently experienced, internal conflicts. Countries such as Brazil and Indonesia – in part due to their vast expanses of remote forests – have limited resources to combat illegal deforestation and subsistence-driven land clearing.

Conducting a root-cause analysis of the specific deforestation and degradation drivers and their particular agents, and then addressing the underlying factors, will greatly increase the chances of a successful REDD+ project and the generation of a verified emission reduction asset.

With an understanding of the location of the world's remaining forests and where the principal deforestation and degradation are occurring, it is now necessary to explore the importance of mitigating such deforestation and degradation and preserving ecosystem services.

CHAPTER 2

The Importance of Mitigating Deforestation and Degradation and Preserving Ecosystem Services

WHAT ARE ECOSYSTEM SERVICES and how valuable are they? Why is mitigating deforestation and degradation important?

Ecosystem services

Ecosystem services, as defined by the Millennium Ecosystem Assessment – a leading publication developed by over 1,350 experts and initiated by the United Nations Secretary General Kofi Annan – are:

> The benefits people obtain from ecosystems. These include provisioning services such as food, water, timber, and fiber; regulating services that affect climate, floods, disease, wastes, and water quality; cultural services that provide recreational, aesthetic, and spiritual benefits; and supporting services such as soil formation, photosynthesis, and nutrient recycling.[11]

Globally, the value of these ecosystem services is estimated to be US$16-54 trillion dollars per year with an average estimated value of US$33 trillion dollars per year.[12] Assuming the average estimated value, global ecosystem services are annually worth more than twice the Gross Domestic Product of the USA.

Ecosystems services are important to every person and every business. These range from food and oxygen production without which life would not be possible, to amenities which make life more enjoyable, such as snorkelling on coral reefs and hiking through pristine forests.

Yet deforestation and degradation are so widespread that they currently contribute approximately 20% of the greenhouse gas (GHG) emissions to the Earth's atmosphere. They account for more emissions than the world's entire collective transport activities, including the fuel combustion from all automobiles, tractors, trucks, and buses.

The world's forests not only provide the climatic benefits of sequestering and storing carbon dioxide emissions, but also a cost-free range of additional ecosystem services such as: erosion control; water cycling, filtration and storage; oxygen production; buffers against storms; medicine and food; and habitat for wildlife.

Erosion control

The roots of trees and other plants hold topsoil in place and help control erosion. When a landscape is deforested, erosion occurs, topsoil is lost, agricultural productivity declines, and in the worst scenarios, mudslides can result.

A Cornell University study published in the journal *Science* suggests 'that about 10% of all the energy used in U.S. agriculture today is spent just to offset the losses of nutrients, water, and crop productivity caused by erosion. [. . .] If the on-site and off-site costs are summed, erosion costs the United States a total of about US$196 ha^{-1}.'[13]

Water cycling, filtration and storage

The roots of trees and other plants also contribute to the world's water cycle, while storing water and freely acting as natural filtration agents. This water storage helps to mitigate the impacts of flooding – localized droughts have been connected to deforestation. For example, 'Indonesia is seeking to establish a 'Green Corridor' in Kalimantan (the Indonesian portion of the island of Borneo), where deforestation is not only fueling greenhouse-gas emissions, but also diminishing river flows, making it difficult in some months to transport goods by barge. Given that transportation by barge costs about US$10 a ton, compared to close to US$60 a ton by road, REDD+ offers a chance to hold down greenhouse-gas emissions while preserving an economically important sector'.[14]

Oxygen production

Alongside ocean plankton, the world's forests are immense producers of oxygen and the Amazon rainforest is commonly referred to as the 'lungs of the planet'.

Buffers against storms

Mangrove forests, which are located in the brackish water near coastlines, help to absorb the energy of hurricanes and typhoons.

The Royal Swedish Academy of Sciences published a study where researchers 'mapped the annual value of coastal wetlands by 1 km x 1 km pixel and by [US] state. The annual value ranged from US$250 to US$51,000 $ha^{-1} yr^{-1}$, with a mean of US$8240 $ha^{-1} yr^{-1}$ (median = US$3230 $ha^{-1} yr^{-1}$) significantly larger than previous estimates. Coastal wetlands in the US were estimated to currently provide US$23.2 billion yr[1] in storm protection services.'[15]

Medicine and food

Tropical forests provide a wide range of medicine and food for both local communities and international consumers. Researchers from the Institute of Economic Botany at the New York Botanical Garden and from the Yale School of Forestry and Environmental Studies estimate:

> Each new drug is worth an average US$94 million to a private drug company and US$449 million to society as a whole. Given recent experience searching for new drugs, we estimate that the higher plants in the world's tropical forests contain about 375 potential pharmaceuticals of which 48 (about one in eight) have already been discovered. Multiplying these values by the number of potential new drugs suggests that a complete collection and screening of all tropical plant species should be worth about US$3–4 billion to a private pharmaceutical company and as much as US$147 billion to society as a whole.[16]

Habitat for wildlife

Dr. E.O. Wilson, the world-renowned Harvard University biologist, states that habitat loss (i.e. anthropogenic deforestation and degradation) is the primary cause of biodiversity loss.[17] Biodiversity is a measure of the health of ecosystems. Wildlife act as natural pollinators and seed dispersers, and play vital roles in the decomposition and recycling of nutrients. They also provide opportunities for ecotourism.

According to Kiplinger, a Washington, DC-based business publication, ecotourism 'captures US$77 billion of the global market and [is] experiencing double-digit gains that are likely to accelerate as concern about global warming rises'.[18]

With all these ecosystem services in mind, it is clearly important to reverse the trend of tropical deforestation. While many mechanisms have tried to arrest deforestation – from legislation to prevent importation of illegal timber to structuring of debt-for-nature swaps – the world is still losing tropical forests at an alarming rate. To counteract this trend, REDD+ is developing as an innovative forest conservation mechanism that has the potential to create value for standing forests and a platform for business sustainability.

....

CHAPTER 3

What is REDD+ and How to Use It as a Tool for Accelerating Business Sustainability

WHAT EXACTLY IS REDD+ and how can it be used as a tool for accelerating business sustainability?

The definition and origins of REDD+

REDD is an acronym that stands for Reducing Emissions from Deforestation and Degradation. According to the United Nations (UN) REDD Programme, REDD is described as 'an effort to create a financial value for the carbon stored in forests, offering incentives for developing countries to reduce emissions from forested lands and invest in low-carbon paths to sustainable development'.[1] The '+' designates the additional activities of forest conservation, sustainable forest management and the enhancement of carbon stocks.

Although REDD and REDD+ are UN terms, REDD and REDD+ projects are being developed in the voluntary carbon markets and in these schemes might be eligible in compliance carbon markets such as the California Emissions Trading Scheme.

Deforestation and degradation can either be planned (e.g. a logging concession is granted) or unplanned (e.g. illegal logging or cattle ranching by local communities without legal title) and take place in either mosaic (alongside population centers) or frontier landscapes (newly accessible forests). Essentially a baseline scenario of deforestation and degradation is established and if project activities are successfully implemented to mitigate such deforestation and degradation, the potential GHG emissions saved can be quantified and sold as verified emission reduction credits.

With this in mind, REDD initially gained traction as a demonstration project in Bolivia. This project, located at the Noel Kempff Mercado National Park, was launched in 1997 by The Nature Conservancy, the Bolivian Government and a local NGO called Friends of Nature Foundation with financial support from American Electric Power, BP Amoco, and PacifiCorp. In addition, Winrock International was instrumental in conducting the technical measurements of the project's biomass and deforestation projections. While there are some notable problems with the Noel Kempff project, this demonstration scheme helped set REDD in motion.[19]

In May 2005 the Coalition for Rainforest Nations was formed and during the 11th United Nations Framework Convention on Climate Change (UNFCCC) Conference of the Parties (COP) in Montreal during December 2005, REDD was officially placed back on the agenda as a potentially viable policy option.[20]

REDD was further refined during the COP-13 in December 2007 with the Bali Action Plan which called for:

- Policy approaches and positive incentives on issues relating to reducing emissions from deforestation and forest degradation in developing countries; and the role of conservation, sustainable management of forests and enhancement of forest carbon stocks in developing countries.

- All Parties to collectively aim at halting forest cover loss in developing countries by 2030 at the latest and reducing gross deforestation in developing countries by at least 50 per cent by 2020 compared to current levels.[20]

As a result of this increasing clarity on policy, Merrill Lynch and Carbon Conservation shortly thereafter (in February 2008) announced their partnership towards financing, developing, and monetizing the first ever validated REDD project within the Ulu Masen Ecosystem of Aceh Province in Indonesia to the Climate, Community and Biodiversity Standard.[21]

For an additional explanation, see **http://www.youtube.com/watch?feature =player_embedded&v=D0WeGw3h2yU** for an introductory video on REDD+.

A tool for business sustainability

REDD+ can provide a significant tool for business sustainability including, but not limited to: mitigating global greenhouse gas emissions while reducing business risk to a changing climate; as part of a firm's philanthropic work; a mechanism to increase consumer loyalty; benefitting upstream local communities and ecosystem services; enhancing corporate social responsibility image and upholding corporate principles; providing unique marketing opportunities and product positioning through private-sector support of charismatic REDD+ projects.

Mitigating global GHG emissions while reducing business risk to a changing climate

All companies are responsible for the generation of greenhouse gas emissions and all companies will be impacted by global climate change.

WHAT IS REDD+ AND HOW TO USE IT AS A TOOL
FOR ACCELERATING BUSINESS SUSTAINABILITY

Companies, whether for a voluntary initiative to reduce GHG emissions or due to a regulatory requirement, can support REDD+ projects.

Supporting REDD+ projects is important in mitigating climate change because all companies are exposed to unique business risks due to a changing climate. For example, droughts and changing rain patterns will impact the underlying assets of timber management companies, paper product businesses, and agricultural firms. Increased storms will threaten the exposure of insurance companies, beachfront hotels, and property management firms. Rising sea levels and decreasing forest cover will further destabilize many non-OECD countries and limit business opportunities in emerging markets.

For example, the German insurance company Allianz acquired a 10% share in the REDD+ project developer Wildlife Works Carbon LLC on 13 October 2011. As stated on Allianz's website:

> In addition to Allianz's voluntary commitment to reduce carbon emissions from its business operations, from 2012 onwards Allianz will neutralize its remaining emissions by directly investing in carbon projects that generate certificates. As only some of the certificates will be required to ensure Allianz's carbon neutrality, the rest can be sold to generate a financial return. This creates a direct incentive for the company to intensify its emission reduction efforts. Carbon investments are thus not just a voluntary means of becoming carbon-neutral, but also a viable business case for Allianz. Investments undertaken in 2011 included:
>
> **Wildlife Works Carbon LLC (WWC)**
> Allianz is furthering forest protection in developing and emerging

countries through the acquisition of a 10 percent share in WWC, an organization that develops Reducing Emissions from Deforestation and Forest Degradation (REDD) projects. The first project is a 208,000 hectare [513,760 acres] forest in South-East Kenya, which acts as a corridor between two national parks. During the 30-year lifetime of this project, up to 36 million metric tons of carbon dioxide emissions will be avoided, generating the equivalent number of carbon credits. By investing in WWC, Allianz is highlighting REDD projects as an attractive investment option, since they combine a high level of social and ecological responsibility with competitive returns for investors.[22]

Philanthropic work

Many firms undertake philanthropic work, whether it is via the establishment of a corporate foundation or through the support of external nonprofit organizations. A portion of such philanthropic work can be dedicated to supporting REDD+ projects.

For example, the Bank of America Charitable Fund has a publicly stated goal of donating a total of US$50 million over 10 years to support nonprofit organizations working on climate change and specifically a US$2 million grant was given to The Nature Conservancy for forest conservation projects in Brazil, Indonesia, and China.[23]

Although not specifically a REDD+ project, Goldman Sachs donated a 735,000 acre (297,571 hectares) tract of land in southern Chile to the Wildlife Conservation Society for the creation of a nature reserve.[24]

Increasing consumer loyalty

Consumers are increasingly aware of the impact of their consumption patterns on the natural environment. This can be demonstrated by the expansion of green products and certifications such as the United States Department of Agriculture certified organic foods, forest stewardship certified (FSC) paper products, Leadership in Energy and Environmental Design (LEED) buildings, and fair trade certified consumer goods. Businesses are able to increase consumer loyalty in part through the support of REDD+ projects.

Benefitting upstream local communities and ecosystem services

A synergy of benefitting upstream local communities – for example within the communities that work for a company's manufacturing facilities – and preserving ecosystem services, can be garnered through supporting REDD+ projects. This can help create goodwill among host governments and communities. An example of this is Puma, which has developed an environmental profit and loss statement to account for the environmental impacts throughout its supply chain.[25]

Enhancing corporate social responsibility image and upholding corporate principles

Many companies have corporate social responsibility (CSR) principles and supporting REDD+ projects offers a mechanism for companies to enhance this CSR image and uphold corporate principles.

This can improve employee recruitment and retention, assist with maintaining and acquiring key accounts, and promote goodwill among host countries and communities, etc.

Providing unique marketing opportunities and product positioning through private-sector support of charismatic REDD+ projects

Carbonfund.org's Carbon*Free*® Product certification and the Carbon-Neutral Company's CarbonNeutral® certification offer unique marketing opportunities for companies which voluntarily measure and offset the lifecycle GHG emissions of a given product.

Wildlife Works Carbon LLC, a pioneering firm which developed the first ever validated and verified REDD+ project, has provided the unique opportunity for firms to source sustainable organic cotton and simultaneously support REDD+ projects.[26]

CHAPTER 4

Business Case Studies and REDD+ Best Practices

REDD+ social, environmental, and financial best practices

THERE ARE NOW A CONSOLIDATED HANDFUL of forest carbon project standards – including for REDD+ projects – that have been established by leading experts. Whether you are developing your own REDD+ project or supporting a third-party REDD+ project, it is vitally important that they are developed according to established international carbon certification standards. These certification standards are important because they ensure projects are:

- Real

- Additional

- Verifiable

- Measureable

- Permanent

An article on recommendations for incorporating the additional characteristics of insured, secured, and preferred into forest carbon projects, can be found here: **http://http://www.ecosystemmarketplace.com/pages/dynamic/article.page.php?page_id=7558&section=home.**

Certification standards also add credibility to projects, increase their sustainability and investability, and ensure scientifically robust quantifications.
These certification standards include, but are not limited to:

- American Carbon Registry (ACR) – **http://americancarbonregistry.org**

- Climate Action Reserve (CAR) – **http://www.climateactionreserve.org**

- The Gold Standard – **http://www.cdmgoldstandard.org**

- Verified Carbon Standard (VCS) – **http://v-c-s.org**

Standards – which can be paired with those mentioned above – that
ensure a REDD+ project is incorporating community and biodiversity
co-benefits include:

- Climate, Community and Biodiversity Standard (CCBS) – **http://
www.climate-standards.org**

- Plan Vivo – **http://www.planvivo.org**

- REDD+ Social & Environmental Standards – **http://www.redd-
standards.org**

- Social Carbon – **http://www.socialcarbon.org**

These additional certifications are important because they ensure
projects result in net positive community and biodiversity impacts; engage
stakeholders and allow communities to provide free, prior and informed
consent; and have biodiversity and community impact monitoring plans.
These attributes will help mitigate risk (e.g. reduce potential of negative
publicity) as well as increasing the likelihood of the project's success, its
permanence, and the ultimate delivery of the underlying asset.

In fact, many investors will only support REDD+ projects that have an additional certification (i.e. see Code REDD below) and buyers are often willing to pay a premium on such projects that ensure additional community and biodiversity benefits.[27]

It is important to note that projects are initially audited by an independent firm (known as validation) to a certification standard and then such projects are periodically audited (known as verification) to determine the appropriate number of verified emission reductions (VERs) to be issued to the project's registry account.

Upon initial validation, a project will have an ex-ante or forecasted quantity of emission reduction credits. Upon verification, a project will have ex-post VERs issued to the project and VERs can be traded in a similar manner to other assets (for example, via exchanges or bilateral purchase agreements).

A few registries and trading exchanges for VERs, including for REDD+ projects, are:

- APX Verified Carbon Standard (VCS) Registry – **http://www.vcs registry.com**

- Carbon Trade Exchange – **http://carbontradexchange.com**

- Markit Environmental Registry – **http://www.markit.com/sites/ en/products/environmental/markit-environmental-registry.page**

Furthermore, there are several associations working either exclusively on REDD+ or in part on REDD+ projects. Such associations include:

- Climate Markets & Investment Association (CMIA) – **http://www. cmia.net**

- Code REDD – http://www.coderedd.org

- International Emissions Trading Scheme (IETA) – http://www.ieta.org

Code REDD, CMIA, and IETA have different audiences yet all garner widespread corporate support with members ranging from international advisory and investment firms to utilities and corporations producing consumer goods.

CMIA is 'an international trade association representing firms that finance, invest in, and provide enabling support to activities that reduce emissions'.[28] Corporate members include carbon market participants along with international consulting, insurance, investment, and law firms such as: Althelia Climate Fund, Bank of America Merrill Lynch, Deutsche Bank, Hunton & Williams, ING, JPMorgan, KPMG, McGuireWoods, Munich Re, Norton Rose Group, PricewaterhouseCoopers LLP, and Wildlife Works Carbon, LLC.

Code REDD 'offers an innovative solution to global deforestation by connecting socially responsible companies with high-quality forest conservation projects'.[29] Thus, Code REDD is specifically focused on engaging companies committed to supporting REDD+ projects. Current corporate champions of Code REDD are Allianz SE, Eneco, ENTEGA, Nedbank, and PPR. Code REDD also has many informative videos (**http://www.coderedd.org/see-all-videos/**) on REDD+ and Corporate Champions.

IETA is '*open to companies, business organizations and affiliated national and regional trading associations. Current Members include: greenhouse gas emitters, verifiers, certifiers, auditors, investors, insurers, traders, brokers, financial and commodity exchanges and other companies serving the greenhouse gas emissions trading market in developed, emerging economies and developing countries*'.[30]

In contrast to CMIA, IETA has more members and although some firms (e.g. Bank of America Merrill Lynch and PricewaterhouseCoopers LLP) are members of both organizations, IETA has more companies facing regulated caps on their emissions. Corporate members of IETA include: American Electric Power, Baker & McKenzie, British Petroleum, Chevron, Citigroup, ConocoPhillips, Dow Chemical Company, Duke Energy, Eneco, Ernst & Young, Goldman Sachs International, Holcim, International Paper, KPMG, Mitsubishi Corporation, Petrobras, Rio Tinto, Toyota Motor Marketing Europe, and Wildlife Works Carbon LLC.

Other less-REDD+ focused associations include:

- Business for Innovative Climate & Energy Policy and Investor Network on Climate Risk (INCR), projects of Ceres – **http://www.ceres.org/bicep**

- Carbon Disclosure Project – **https://www.cdproject.net/en-US/Pages/HomePage.aspx**

- Climate Bonds Initiative – **http://climatebonds.net**

- Network for Sustainable Financial Markets – **http://www.sustainablefinancialmarkets.net**

Financial Standards

In addition to carbon and co-benefit certification standards, REDD+ project developers and investors should seek the highest level of financial transparency and practice business ethics. This includes valuing REDD+ transactions on the balance sheet, at fair value, and within a firm's inventory.

Financial criteria for REDD+ projects include, but are not limited to:

- A transparent, auditable business plan with audited annual financial statements that abide by US Financial Accounting Standards Board (FASB) and/or the International Accounting Standards Board (IASB) guidance.

It is also worth exploring government financing, including from national governments such as Germany, Norway, and the United States. The German Agency for International Cooperation (Gesellschaft für Internationale Zusammenarbeit or GIZ), in collaboration with the Laos Government, provided financial support to the Indonesian-based firm Forest Carbon to 'carry out a jurisdiction-wide, wall-to-wall REDD+ analysis [in Laos], identifying potential investment opportunities for private companies interested in forest conservation and ecosystem restoration'.[31]

In addition, the Government of Norway has committed more than US$2 billion in support for REDD+ activities in the host countries of Brazil, Guyana, Indonesia, and Tanzania.[32]

The United States Government has also provided direct and indirect support for international REDD+ projects including providing political risk insurance, offering technical forestry expertise, and financial backing. For example,

- The US Department of Treasury's Fiscal Year 2012 included 'Tropical Forest Conservation Act (TFCA) request of US$15 million for sovereign debt restructuring, while generating funds to support forest conservation' and 'Requests for the GEF include US$144 million to provide incremental funding for projects that provide global environmental benefits, such as reducing greenhouse gas pollution and conserving biodiversity.'

- The Overseas Private Investment Corporation 'Board approval for a US$ 40 million investment in a community based REDD+ and forest carbon private equity fund.'

- The first political risk insurance contract for a REDD+ project that will protect 64,318 hectares of forest in Cambodia and sequester approximately 8.7 million $mtCO_2e$.[33]

Furthermore, emerging financial standards which are relevant for REDD+ projects include:

- Accounting guidance provided by FASB and IASB

- Possibly the International Swap Dealers Association

- Chartered Financial Analyst (CFA) Institute Codes
    - Code of Ethics & Standards of Professional Conduct
    - Asset Manager Code of Professional Conduct
    - Endowments Code of Conduct
    - Global Investment Performance Standards (GIPS)

- Insurance mechanisms

The Code of Ethics and Standards of Professional Conduct are the 'ethical benchmark for investment professionals around the globe, regardless of job title, cultural differences, or local laws'.[34]

The Asset Manager Code of Professional Conduct is the 'global standard of conduct for investment managers to affirm their commitment to ethical principles that put client interests first. Plan Sponsors and other investors can easily identify asset managers that uphold an ethical foundation that resolves conflicts of interest in favor of investors.'[35]

The Code of Conduct for Endowments, Foundations, and Charitable Organizations 'outlines ethical responsibilities for the sound management of longer-term financial assets. Organizations that adopt and incorporate the Code:

- Establish an ethical framework for governing body members

- Show commitment to the best interests of stakeholders and beneficiaries'[36]

GIPS is a 'set of standardized, industry-wide ethical principles that provide investment firms with guidance on how to calculate and report their investment results to prospective clients'.[37]

There are also a suite of insurance mechanisms being developed and applied to the forest carbon markets and specifically to REDD+ projects. The most notable insurance example to date is the Overseas Private Investment Corporation's (OPIC) approval of political risk insurance for a REDD+ project in Cambodia. Essentially, OPIC offers protection against currency inconvertibility, expropriation, and political violence which, as mentioned above, can be particularly important for REDD+ projects being developed in host countries experiencing the highest rates of deforestation.[38]

For an overview of insurance mechanisms tailored to the forest carbon markets, see **http://www.garp.org/risk-news-and-resources/2012/august/ risk-management-trends-in-forest-carbon.aspx?p=1** for an article published by the Global Association of Risk Professionals.

Case studies on ways for businesses to get involved

If your business wants to get involved with a REDD+ project, there are several ways to become engaged. This includes: developing your own

REDD+ project; donating to a nonprofit organization that is supporting REDD+ projects; investing in a company that is developing REDD+ projects; invest directly into a particular REDD+ project; or invest into a pooled fund.

Whether your company is developing its own project or investing into a pooled fund, Figure 1 gives a basic timeline for REDD+ projects:

FIGURE 1. Basic timeline of REDD+ projects

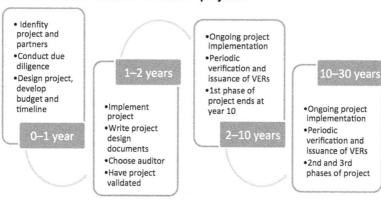

Developing your own REDD+ project

Although it is technically challenging, requires relatively large upfront costs, and will be time-consuming, developing your own REDD+ project can have advantages such as lower costs and larger net profits, greater control over the project, and increased marketing opportunities. This is not recommended for most companies, unless there are logical synergies such as for a pulp and paper firm or a timber management company which already owns forest concessions.

Forest carbon projects follow the same project finance and project development process as other agriculture, forestry and land-use projects (AFOLU) with the added criteria of biodiversity and community co-benefits. Figure 2 gives a basic framework for how to develop a REDD+ project, using the five stages of project management from the Project Management Body of Knowledge (PMBOK):

FIGURE 2. Stages

Stage 1: Initiate

'The process in which it is decided that there is a need for a particular project and then the decision that the project will begin.'[39]

- Identify potential project(s) and partner(s)
- Draft cost–benefit analysis, detailed timeline, and other prefeasibility activities
- Sign legal agreements outlining roles and responsibilities
- Obtain landownership documentation and project maps
- Have rapid deforestation assessment conducted
- Have landownership documents reviewed, counterparty due diligence
- Have project maps reviewed, make sure no overlapping title claims
- Refine estimated budget and revenue forecast
- Decide whether to move forward with project

Stage 2: Plan

'The process in which the scope of the project is developed, including documenting the actions necessary to define, prepare, integrate, and coordinate all subsidiary plans into a project management plan.'[39]

- Choose certification standard; download project design document (PDDs) templates
- Develop request for proposals (RFPs), send out RFPs for any required technical assistance, review proposals, chose firm, and develop services agreement
- Meet with local communities to explain project and seek their insights into project design
- Identify most important social projects/ programs to mitigate deforestation

Stage 3: Execute

'The process in which the necessary actions are performed in order to accomplish the goals that were set in the planning stage.'[39]

- Write draft PDDs and engage project stakeholders
- Undertake technical deforestation baseline development and conduct forest carbon inventory
- Design community impact and biodiversity impact monitoring plans
- Send out RFPs for auditor, review proposals, contract auditor and confirm site visit

Stage 4: Monitor and control

'The process in which the actions performed in the execute stage are supervised, in order to ensure the project is successful in meeting the predetermined goals.'[39]

- Receive results from technical deforestation baseline
- Receive results from forest carbon inventory
- Ongoing engagement with communities and stakeholders
- Submit completed project design documents to auditor

Stage 5: Close

'The process in which the finished product or service is presented, indicating successful completion of the project.'[39]

- Start public comment period and solicit comments
- Undertake site visit with auditors for validation
- Receive findings from auditor; address and close all findings
- Chose registry provider, submit necessary documentation
- Submit finalized project design documents (PDDs)
- Ongoing implementation of social projects and programs to stop deforestation
- Ongoing monitoring, reporting and verification (MRV) of emission reductions
- Undertake firm's exit strategy

Costs

Forest carbon projects, particularly REDD+ projects, do involve a substantial amount of upfront costs ranging from approximately US$350,000 to over US$700,000 per project. This includes major items such as:

- Due diligence and feasibility assessments: US$15,000 to US$25,000

- Legal fees and translation costs: US$25,000 to US$50,000

- Site visits and preparation of project design documents: US$100,000 to US$250,000

- Biodiversity and community impact monitoring plans: US$25,000 to US$75,000

- Technical baseline development and forest inventory work: US$150,000 to US$250,000

- Validation services: US$40,000 to US$80,000

These costs are generally fixed – regardless of the project size and location – and are accrued in the first two years.

Note, these upfront costs do not include the purchasing of land and can vary depending on the capability of internal staff. It is important to note that in many places land cannot be purchased by foreign entities and instead companies may have to obtain a concession (e.g. timber or payment for ecosystem service concession) or lease the land.

Ongoing costs include implementing local social projects and programs – forest patrols of potential deforestation sites, agricultural extension work, land titling to local communities, providing employment opportunities to reduce pressure on forest resources or foregoing clear-cutting operations – along with the monitoring, reporting and verification of reducing emissions and demonstrating positive net benefits to local communities and biodiversity. These ongoing costs can range from approximately US$2 to US$5 per verified emission reduction (VERs).

Revenue

The revenue stream of REDD+ projects is primarily the generation of VERs, otherwise known as carbon offset credits, which are the underlying assets equivalent to reducing one metric tonne of carbon dioxide equivalent emissions ($mtCO_2e$).

To better understand the approximate sales price per VER, the annual volume of international sales, along with the location of buyers and location of projects, see the following resources:

- Ecosystem Marketplace and Bloomberg New Energy Finance's State of the Voluntary Carbon Markets 2011 Report – **http://www. forest-trends.org/publication_details.php?publicationID=2828**

- Ecosystem Marketplace's State of the Forest Carbon Markets 2011 Report – **http://www.forest-trends.org/publication_details. php?publicationID=2963**

- World Bank's State and Trends of the Carbon Market Report 2012 – **http://siteresources.worldbank.org/INTCARBONFINANCE/ Resources/State_and_Trends_2012_Web_Optimized_19035_ Cvr&Txt_LR.pdf**

- Forest Carbon Portal – http://www.forestcarbonportal.com

While the underlying asset is the generation of VERs, there are other potential revenue streams including the generation of additional environmental certificates (e.g. biodiversity credits and water credits), ecotourism opportunities, agroforestry, and locally sourced sustainable forestry products (e.g. improved forestry management or cooperative Brazil nut harvesting).

In addition, there are different compensation schemes. If you are the project developer, you can retain a portion of the VERs to compensate, with a return, your initial investment to cover the costs of starting a REDD+ project. Alternatively if you are investing in another company, another project or a pooled fund, you can consider the following arrangements:

Provide upfront or ongoing financing, in exchange for percentage or fixed quantity of VERs

This percentage or fixed quantity of VERs could be front-loaded in the early years or spread evenly over the REDD+ project lifetime. Your firm should have enough market knowledge and ability to sell VERs if you are contemplating this structure.

Provide upfront or ongoing financing, in exchange for a percentage of ongoing revenue

If your firm is less familiar with the carbon markets, you might want to receive a percentage of ongoing revenue and leave the sale of VERs to another firm.

Provide upfront or ongoing financing, in exchange for a fixed, flat-fee of future revenue

This fixed, flat-fee could be front-loaded in the early years or spread evenly over the REDD+ project lifetime.

Brokerage fees for selling VERs

Typical brokerage fees in the voluntary carbon markets are 3.0–3.5% on gross contract value.

Trade VERs above an agreed-upon minimum price

Instead of participating as a broker in a neutral intermediary position, your firm could take ownership of VERs and receive any profits earned by trading VERs above an agreed upon minimum price.

Cost-plus arrangement to develop project

Rather than providing upfront or ongoing financing, your company might choose to develop a REDD+ project with another firm's financing. Under this structure, your firm could have your accrued costs paid back plus a fixed fee or percentage of costs as compensation.

Management fee to manage pooled fund

As will be described below, there are several pooled funds – such as the Terra Bella Fund – dedicated to REDD+ projects and the management firms receive a management fee from investors.

Use of put or call options

Your firm could consider put or call options by paying an option premium to have the right, but not the obligation, to buy or sell VERs at a certain strike price. If your firm is considering developing its own REDD+ project, a good guidance document developed by Forest Trends and EcoDecisión is called *Building Forest Carbon Projects: Step-by-Step Overview and Guide*.[40]

Donating to a nonprofit organization supporting REDD+ projects

Many local and international nonprofit organizations are actively working on REDD+ activities. This includes NGOs directly leading the origination and development of REDD+ projects to NGOs which support projects from more of a technical or policy angle. Such NGOs include, but are certainly not limited, to:

- Amazon Environmental Research Institute (IPAM) – http://www.ipam.org.br/o-ipam/Sobre-o-IPAM/1

- Carbonfund.org Foundation, Inc. – http://www.carbonfund.org/projects

- Conservation International (CI) – http://www.conservation.org/learn/climate/solutions/mitigation/pages/climate_redd.aspx

- Fauna & Flora International (FFI) – http://www.fauna-flora.org/initiatives/redd/

- The Nature Conservancy (TNC) – http://www.nature.org/our initiatives/urgentissues/global-warming-climate-change/how-we-work/creating-incentives-to-stop-deforestation.xml

- World Resources Institute (WRI) – http://www.wri.org/topics/redd

- World Wildlife Fund (WWF) – http://worldwildlife.org/threats/deforestation

Table 4 provides a list of the top 20 climate change funders in 2008 according to Steven Lawrence, Director of Research for the Foundation Center:

TABLE 4. Top foundations supporting climate change (data from Foundation Center)

	Foundation name	Amount given	Grants given
1	William and Flora Hewlett Foundation	US$548,682,703	91
2	David and Lucile Packard Foundation	US$70,545,985	91
3	Rockefeller Foundation*	US$37,255,400	58
4	Kresge Foundation	US$18,095,000	18
5	Lincy Foundation	US$15,000,000	1
6	Skoll Foundation*	US$13,060,000	4
7	Robert Wood Johnson Foundation	US$10,556,761	7
8	Sea Change Foundation	US$9,355,000	8
9	John D. and Catherine T. MacArthur*	US$9,306,000	20
10	Richard and Rhoda Goldman Fund	US$8,216,000	54
11	Gordon and Betty Moore Foundation*	US$7,550,830	17
12	Ford Foundation	US$7,389,293	37
13	Kendeda Fund	US$7,083,000	20
14	Joyce Foundation	US$6,894,035	19
15	Rockefeller Brothers Fund	US$6,465,580	46
16	California Endowment	US$6,132,499	22
17	Richard King Mellon Foundation	US$5,055,000	2
18	Surdna Foundation	US$4,355,000	40
19	McKnight Foundation	US$3,904,000	6
20	New York Community Trust	US$3,088,000	41

*It is important to note the John D. and Catherine T. MacArthur Foundation was a funding supporter of the Oddar Meanchey REDD Project in Cambodia, the Surdna Foundation funds the Forest Carbon Portal, the Rockefeller Foundation is a donor to the Climate,

Community and Biodiversity Standard, while both the Skoll Foundation and the Gordon and Betty Moore Foundation donated to the State of the Forest Carbon Markets 2012 Report. Thus, it is certainly plausible the remaining top 20 foundations might also consider donating specifically to REDD+ projects. Overall, the top 20 foundations contributed approximately US$798 million dollars and made a total of 602 grants.[41]

Investing in a for-profit company developing REDD+ projects

There are several for-profit companies currently developing REDD+ projects and there are many potential ways for companies to invest in such companies.

As previously mentioned, investments could include a cost-plus arrangement where your company provides start-up costs to be paid back plus a fixed fee, percentage of revenue, or percentage of VERs as compensation.

The purchase of VERs is usually made via a legal, purchase agreement called a Verified Emission Reduction Purchase Agreement (VERPA) or an Emission Reduction Purchase Agreement (ERPA). See **http://www.ieta. org/assets/tradingdocs/cdmerpav.3.0final.doc** for an ERPA template developed by the International Emissions Trading Association (IETA) and **here** for another ERPA template developed by the World Bank.

For-profit firms include:

- CarbonCo, LLC – **http://carboncollc.com**

- Ecosystem Restoration Associates, Inc. – **http://www.eraeco systems.com**

- Forest Carbon Offsets, LLC – **http://www.forestcarbonoffsets.net**

- South Pole Carbon Asset Management – http://www.southpole carbon.com

- Terra Global Capital, LLC – http://www.terraglobalcapital.com

- Wildlife Works Carbon, LLC – http://www.wildlifeworks.com/index. php

Please note this list of for-profit firms is not intended to be an approved or sponsored list, so it will be important for your company to conduct its own know-your-counterparty (KYC) due diligence.

The following are several case studies on how a company can invest into a for-profit firm which is developing REDD+ projects. Note Wildlife Works Carbon LLC was the first company to have a validated and verified REDD+ project so the majority of these case studies are based on this firm's experience.

PPR invests in Wildlife Works Carbon LLC. PPR, which owns notable luxury brands such as Gucci, Yves Saint Laurent, Puma, and Volcom, bought a 5% stake in the REDD+ project developer Wildlife Works Carbon LLC.[42] Part of PPR's stated five-year plan involves:

Reducing our carbon emissions, waste and water usage resulting from the production of products and services by 25%, while accounting for the growth of our business. All remaining emissions from scope 1 and scope 2 of the Greenhouse Gas Protocol will be offset annually. PPR will continue to partner with offset programs that contribute to the welfare of the community and the conservation of biodiversity in its regions of operations. Carbon credits were purchased from Wildlife Works' leading REDD (Reduced

Emissions from Deforestation and Degradation) offsetting project in Kenya which is the world's first Voluntary Carbon Standard (VCS) validated and verified REDD program. Wildlife Works' project directly: reduces greenhouse gas emissions by protecting threatened forests that are essential in mitigating climate change; improves the quality of life for local communities; and conserves endangered wildlife. Furthermore, PPR has acquired a 5% stake in Wildlife Works Carbon, LLC. Aside from already having 500,000 hectares [1,235,000 acres] under protection, Wildlife Works Carbon, LLC has a prospective project pipeline of several million hectares of natural forests around the world. The voluntary carbon market is placed for growth and potential for return could exceed the original investment by multiple times. Additionally, the investment fulfills one of PPR HOME's primary goals, to invest in for-profit businesses that incorporate biodiversity conservation and social concerns into their business model, resulting in net-positive social and environmental impacts. PPR, via PPR HOME, will hold a seat on Wildlife Works' Management Committee and joins a group of reputable corporate partners and shareholders in the company. PPR now has an active role in supporting Wildlife Works' aims to secure 5 million hectares [12.35 million acres] of native forest over the next 3 years and to protect them for a minimum of 20 years with an expected 25 million tonnes of CO_2 emissions mitigated annually, while supporting human wellbeing and improved livelihoods for local communities.[42]

Furthermore, the acquisition by PPR of Wildlife Work Carbon LLC's REDD+ credits was partially facilitated by Nedbank, a South African bank.[43]

BNP Paribas and Wildlife Works Carbon LLC. BNP Paribas, a global investment bank registered in France, was involved in one of – if not the – largest REDD+ commitments to date. Essentially, BNP Paribas structured a US$50 million line of credit with Wildlife Works Carbon LLC for project finance and BNP Paribas also secured a call option on up to 1.25 million REDD+ credits from Wildlife Works Carbon LLC's Kasigau Corridor REDD+ Project in southern Kenya.[44]

As explained by Christian del Valle, then-Director at BNP Paribas's Environmental Markets division:

> *The structure worked because it provided the necessary capital to scale up the activity, while at the same time not placing an unrealistic or unworkable obligation on the project implementer or land-use rights owners . . . Clearly, among the most important . . . lessons is that it is absolutely crucial to design a structure that allows for all stakeholders to have their needs met and maintain aligned interests over the long term.[45]*

Ecosystem Restoration Associates, a publicly traded company. Ecosystem Restoration Associates (ERA), which is currently developing REDD+ projects[46] in British Columbia and the Democratic Republic of Congo, is a publicly traded company on the TSX-V Exchange of Canada.[47] Thus, both individuals and businesses can invest into ERA by purchasing publicly traded shares.

Historically one of the largest ERA shareholders was the Forest Carbon Group (FCG) which is affiliated with the German-based energy and infrastructure company HEAG Südhessische Energie AG (HSE). In the press release confirming FCG purchased 7.36 million common shares, the equivalent to 29.9% of ERA, the Director of FCG and Chief Financial Officer of HSE Holger Mayer stated:

> The foundation of Forest Carbon Group and the strategic stake it has taken in ERA is another consequent step for HSE to move from being part of the problem of the climate crisis to be part of the solution. Afforestation of natural forests and forest protection are indispensable to solving the climate crisis, maintaining biodiversity and guaranteeing the sustainable existence of humanity. Together, FCG and ERA will be able to offer access to large scale, high quality forest projects that fit the demands of companies in need of compensating emissions that are still unavoidable for either technical or economical reasons.[48]

In addition, ERA has acquired the clean energy firm Offsetters Clean Technology and the greenhouse gas mitigation firm Carbon Credit Corp. Such an acquisition provides some insights into how other firms can acquire a firm involved in REDD+ projects.[49]

Although limited on publicly available details, ERA also entered into a joint venture with Wildlife Works Carbon LLC on the nearly 300,000 hectare (741,000 acres) Mai Ndombe REDD+ project which is reported to be the first in the Democratic Republic of Congo.[50]

Investing in a particular project

Instead of investing in a particular for-profit firm, which might be developing several REDD+ projects or several different types of carbon reduction and clean energy projects, your company could also explore investing directly into one particular project.

There are several REDD+ projects which are in the project implementation stage and such projects can be identified by reviewing the various project design documents at the following websites:

- American Carbon Registry – **https://acr2.apx.com/myModule/rpt/ myrpt.asp?r=111**

- Climate Action Reserve – **https://thereserve2.apx.com/myModule/ rpt/myrpt.asp?r=111**

- Climate, Community and Biodiversity Standard Projects – **http:// www.climate-standards.org/category/projects/**

- Verified Carbon Standard's VCS Project Database – **http://www. vcsprojectdatabase.org**

Other search engines to identify early-stage projects or projects currently under development include:

- The Forest Carbon Project Portal of Ecosystem Marketplace's Forest Carbon Portal – **http://www.forestcarbonportal.com/projects**

- eCO2market (paid subscription required) – **http://eco2data.co**

- The Carbon Project Manager and Carbon Project Manager North America databases from Thomson Reuters' Point Carbon (paid subscription required) – **http://thomsonreuters.com/products_ services/financial/financial_products/commodities/energy/ research_forecasts/point_carbon_project_manager/** and **http:// thomsonreuters.com/products_services/financial/financial_ products/commodities/energy/research_forecasts/point_ carbon_project_manager_north_america/**

- The World Bank's Project Portfolio – https://wbcarbonfinance. org/Router.cfm?Page=ProjPort&ItemID=24702

International corporations – such as Thomson Reuters's acquisition of Point Carbon and the eCO2market subscription by E.ON Climate and Renewables North America, a subsidiary of the UK energy firm E.ON – are involved in this sector.

The following are a few case studies of firms which have specifically invested into a particular REDD+ project.

Marriott International and the Juma Project. Marriott International committed US$2 million to the Juma Project, a large-scale REDD+ project in the State of Amazonas, Brazil. The Juma Project is being implemented in conjunction with the state government and the Amazonas Sustainable Foundation. Essentially, Marriott 'measured its electricity and gas consumption in guest rooms and public spaces at nearly 1,000 managed hotels worldwide, as well as at its headquarters building and regional offices' and will reduce such emissions via its support of the Juma Project.[51]

Arne Sorenson, the President and Chief Operating Officer of Marriott and the co-chair of Marriott's Green Council, explained Marriott's motivation to get involved with the Juma Project during an interview with SmartPlanet of CBS Interactive:

One of my best friends is an Amazonian scholar, and he had a book-launching party. The governor of the state of Amazonas was there, and we were sitting around, chatting informally, and he said to me, we'd sure like your help with the Amazon. A year-and-a-half later, Marriott had an agreement with the Amazonas Sustainable Foundation (FAS). The notion was, how do you come up with a project which is very concrete, which our customers could see and touch if they wanted to? It's not some intangible idea on carbon offsets. It's a million and a half acres – roughly the size of Delaware – in the Amazon where we can say, that's the land we're protecting. Customers can see it on Google Earth, or they could go visit it.[52]

Merrill Lynch and reducing carbon emissions from deforestation in the Ulu Masen Ecosystem Project. The Ulu Masen Ecosystem Project is a 750,000 acre (303,644 hectare) REDD+ project in Aceh, Indonesia and Merrill Lynch was selected as a strategic partner tasked with 'raising equity for a 100-million-ton, for-profit avoided deforestation project'.[21]

The Global Head of Carbon Emissions at Merrill Lynch, Abyd Karmali, was quoted in a press released picked up by the Spain–US Chamber of Commerce:

The benefits from this project extend beyond carbon to include community economic development, poverty alleviation, species protection and biodiversity conservation. It will also make a significant contribution to the emerging knowledge base on how to commercially structure avoided deforestation projects and will therefore be an important input to the U.N. climate change negotiations. According to the IPCC, land use change and deforestation represents 18 to 25 percent of annual global greenhouse gas emissions. We look forward to working together with Carbon Conservation, Fauna & Flora International and other partners on this landmark project.[53]

American Electric Power, BP-Amoco, PacifiCorp and the Noel Kempff REDD+ Project. The Government of Bolivia, along with American Electric

Power, BP-Amoco, and PacifiCorp, invested in the previously mentioned first ever REDD+ project located adjacent to the Noel Kempff Mercado National Park in Bolivia.[54]

Investing in pooled fund dedicated to REDD+

As opposed to investing in one particular project, the opportunity to invest in a pooled fund dedicated to REDD+ projects is now becoming a possibility.

Investing in a pooled fund offers many potential advantages. A pooled fund provides diversification across projects and geography, while simultaneously reducing one's risk exposures. In addition, there are economies of scale when developing several REDD+ projects. Businesses with an interest in investing into pooled funds dedicated to REDD+ projects should be involved in alternative investments with a particular focus on socially responsible attributes and be comfortable with higher risk versus return tradeoffs.

Below are a few of the publicly disclosed REDD+ pooled funds that have either closed or are currently seeking investments.

Terra Bella Carbon Fund. The Terra Bella Carbon Fund, which was created and will be managed by Terra Global Capital, is currently seeking investments.[55] The Terra Bella Carbon Fund has a capitalization goal of US$100 million and has already secured a US$40 million anchor investment and political insurance from the Overseas Private Investment Corporation.[56]

The World Bank. The World Bank has several funds, some of which provide project finance and others which provide technical assistance to national REDD+ initiatives. Such funds include the Forest Carbon Partnership Facility (FCPF), which manages the Readiness Mechanism Fund and the Carbon Fund.[57]

In addition, the BioCarbon Fund has also been established. As described by the World Bank:

> The World Bank has mobilized a fund to demonstrate projects that sequester or conserve carbon in forest and agro-ecosystems. The Fund, a public/private initiative administered by the World Bank, aims to deliver cost-effective emission reductions, while promoting biodiversity conservation and poverty alleviation. The Fund is composed of two Tranches: Tranche One started operations in May 2004, has a total capital of US$53.8 million; Tranche Two was operationalized in March 2007 and has a total capital of US$36.6 million. Both Tranches are closed to new fund participation.
>
> The BioCarbon Fund can consider purchasing carbon from a variety of land use and forestry projects; the portfolio includes Afforestation and Reforestation, Reducing Emissions from Deforestation and Degradation and is exploring innovative approaches to agricultural carbon.
>
> The BioCarbon Fund is a public/private initiative established as a trust fund administered by the World Bank. The World Bank, as Trustee, oversees the BioCarbon Fund's management and appoints a Fund Manager and a Fund Management Unit. This unit is part of the World Bank's Carbon Finance Unit and draws on the World Bank's experience with carbon finance.[58]

Biocarbon Group Pte Limited. The BioCarbon Group Pte Limited – which is different to the aforementioned BioCarbon Fund administered by the World Bank – is a pooled investment by several investors to support REDD+ projects. Initiated by Macquarie Bank, which is based in Australia, and the international nonprofit organization Fauna and Flora International, the BioCarbon Group Pte Limited has been launched by a US$25 million investment from Macquarie Bank, the International Finance Corporation,[59] and Global Forestry Partners.[60]

Althelia Ecosphere Fund. The Althelia Ecosphere Fund has created the Althelia Climate Fund which intends to deploy:

approximately €200 million [approximately US$255 million] across a portfolio of between 20 and 25 investments that will be engaged within the next 3 years. The Fund will mainly target sustainable land use and forest carbon by allocating at least two-thirds of its commitments to REDD+, but may also explore other types of investments provided they encompass demonstrable GHG reductions accompanied by social and environmental value at the local level.[61]

The cofounders of the Althelia Ecosphere Fund are Christian del Valle and Sylvain Goupille, who both worked at BNP Paribas, the French investment bank that provided US$50 million in investment to Wildlife Works Carbon LLC's REDD+ projects. To date, the Althelia Ecosphere has engaged BNP Paribas, along with Allianz Climate Solutions, the Church of Sweden, Conservation International, the Dutch development finance institution FMO, and Pact.[61]

In addition, Conservation International has publicly committed US$1.35 million of upfront bridge financing to the Althelia Ecosphere

Fund,[62] while as of May 2011 the European Investment Bank was considering an investment into the Althelia Ecosphere Fund of approximately €20 million (approximately US$25.5 million).[63]

Due diligence questions if investing or donating to REDD+

Risks, and how they are managed, will largely depend on the particular REDD+ landownership type, the host country, and your firm's preferred risk mitigation strategies.

From the national to the local level, landowner types for REDD+ projects can be:

- Programs that are nationwide such as the Programa Socio Bosque in Ecuador. – **http://sociobosque.ambiente.gob.ec/**.

- Nationally protected areas and other nationwide REDD+ programs (e.g. UN-REDD and World Bank Forest Carbon Partnership Facility countries).

- Financially linking provincial programs across sovereign boundaries such as the emerging MAP initiative with Madre de Dios-Peru, Acre-Brazil, and Pando-Bolivia.

- Provincial programs (e.g. Governors Climate and Forest Task Force– **http://www.gcftaskforce.org/**).

- Privately owned property.

- Concessionaires (for example, timber, mining, and natural gas concessions).

- Indigenous peoples or forest-dependent rural communities with or without titled land.

Generally speaking, privately owned property and concessionaires (assuming concessions grant ecosystem service attributes) will be easier for REDD+ projects than lands with indigenous peoples or forest-dependent rural communities without title.

The following are a variety of due diligence questions your company should consider when investing or donating to a REDD+ project, company, or fund.

Regional, jurisdictional, country and political

To begin, your company should consider if there are particular regions or countries in which you would like to support or develop a REDD+ project. For example, is there a particular new emerging market that your company would like to enter?

Many of these questions are similar whether you are developing a REDD+ project or setting up a manufacturing facility or a new regional headquarters. Consider the following:

- What are the chances of regional or country-level instability?

- What are the chances of appropriation and/or creeping appropriation?

- What is the extent of corruption and how effective are the courts and law enforcement?

- Would changes in the country's tax, regulatory, or currency policies impact the project?

Macroeconomic and currency risks

Macroeconomic and currency risks will be particularly important if your company decides to develop a REDD+ project or invest into a particular project. In contrast if your company invests in a pooled fund or a company with diverse projects, then such macroeconomic and currency risks can be mitigated. A few questions your firm should analyze include:

- What type of taxes (e.g. capital gains, property, etc.) relate to the project?

- What insurance products (e.g. liability, general contractor, errors and omissions) exist?

- Are there signs the host country has fiscal and/or monetary problems?

- Are there any relevant tariffs, quotas, licensing requirements, or capital controls?

- Does your company have an exit strategy to successfully divest from the project?

- How would an appreciation or depreciation of the local currency vis-à-vis the US dollar or Euro impact the project(s)?

Information risk

Information risks exist for all businesses and projects. In addition to making sure translations are properly done and that all contracts are in place:

- How does one determine clear landownership? Are landowner documents valid?

- How might delays in receiving information (i.e. due to translation, limited technology, spatial distance, etc.) impact the project?

- How might a lack of information (i.e. such as no satellite imagery, lack of biodiversity and community studies, etc.) impact the project?

- Will intellectual property rights be respected?

REDD+ project level

All land-use projects – whether it is a forest carbon project, a logging concession, or the foreign acquisition of land for agriculture and livestock operations – need to take into account local, on-the-ground conditions. For example, what are the chances of extreme weather events, geological risk, or pest infestation and how will climate change impact the project? Some due diligence questions more specific to the REDD+ project level are:

- Have communities given free, prior, and informed consent?

- Do the implementation partners have experience developing REDD+ projects and a long-term relationship with on-the-ground partners?

- What are the chances of a reversal in carbon stocks? Said differently, how sufficient will the local social programs and projects be at stopping deforestation? What if market forces change and increase the value of alternative land uses?

- What, and to what extent, are the drivers of deforestation?

- What will the price of VERs be, particularly REDD+ VERs, over the 30-year time period?

- Is the market for REDD+ VERs liquid? How large will the demand be for these VERs?

CHAPTER 5

The Future of REDD+

THE FUTURE OF REDD+ IS COMPLICATED, but it provides a promising mechanism for financing forest conservation. The following will briefly explore the potential future demand and supply of REDD+ projects, along with future financing arrangements.

Future demand for REDD+

Emerging demand for REDD+ projects will come from voluntary donations, alternative investment firms, and companies driven by compliance obligations. See the previously mentioned State of the Forest Carbon Markets 2012 Report for a discussion of the voluntary actors currently supporting REDD+ projects. With respect to alternative investment firms, see the previously mentioned for-profit REDD+ developers and the pooled funds dedicated to REDD+.

If the USA – either through an integrated regional approach or via a federally implemented cap-and-trade system – develops a mechanism to support REDD-based carbon reduction projects, there will be great promise for REDD+. While the chances for market-based, federal US legislation are currently unlikely, many national and subnational entities – such as the State of California – are currently moving forward with emissions trading schemes.

A case in point is the subnational Memorandum of Understanding (MOU) signed by California (United States), Chiapas (Mexico), and Acre (Brazil) on 16 November 2010. A few key aspects of this MOU relating to REDD+ projects include:

Recognizing further the importance of focusing on issues of common interest between the Parties, such as reducing greenhouse gas emissions in the forest sector by preserving standing forests and sequestering additional carbon through the restoration and reforestation of degraded lands and forest, and through improved forest management practices;

Recognizing further that the Governors' Climate and Forests (GCF) Task Force is a unique subnational collaboration between 14 states and provinces from the United States, Brazil, Indonesia, Nigeria, and Mexico that seeks to integrate Reducing Emissions from Deforestation and Forest Degradation (REDD) and other forest carbon activities into emerging greenhouse gas (GHG) compliance regimes in the United States and elsewhere. As such, the GCF represents an important foundation for identifying enhanced partnerships.

ARTICLE 2 The Parties will coordinate efforts and promote collaboration for environmental management, scientific and technical investigation, and capacity building, through cooperative efforts focused particularly on:

a. Reducing greenhouse gas emissions from deforestation and land degradation – otherwise known as "REDD" – and sequestration of additional carbon through the restoration and reforestation of degraded lands and forests, and through improved forest management practices.

b. Developing recommendations together to ensure that forest-sector emissions reductions and sequestrations, from activities undertaken at the sub-national level, will be real, additional, quantifiable, permanent, verifiable and enforceable, and capable of being recognized in compliance mechanisms of each party's state.[64]

There are also numerous other emerging emissions trading schemes around the world including those in Australia, China, and South Korea, which might create a demand opportunity for REDD+ projects.

Furthermore, the private sector – whether through industry associations such as Code REDD and the International Emissions Trading Association or forward-thinking sustainability leaders such as Puma and Marriott – can help drive REDD+ demand.

Future supply of REDD+

Potential supply of future projects will probably include countries currently hosting REDD+ projects, along with countries that are involved with REDD+ initiatives such as those of the United Nations or World Bank, countries experiencing relatively high deforestation trends, and countries with significant levels of carbon stocks.

Thus, countries getting involved with international REDD+ initiatives with the potential to reverse high rates of deforestation and to mitigate GHG emissions from forests with high levels of carbon stocks seem to be likely candidates.

In terms of above-ground and below-ground carbon stocks in living forest biomass, the State of the World's Forests 2011 Report was very sparse on

TABLE 5. Carbon stocks and deforestation (FAO data)[65]

	Country	2010 carbon stock (millions)		Country	Tonnes per hectare in 2010		Country	Annual change rate 2000–2010 (1000 tonnes)
1	Brazil	62,607	1	Micronesia	318	1	Brazil	-270
2	Russia	32,500	2	Palau	264	2	Indonesia	-217
3	Dem. Republic of Congo	19,639	3	Suriname	214	3	Nigeria	-47
4	USA	19,308	4	French Guiana	204	4	Canada	-41
5	Canada	13,908	5	Guadeloupe	195	5	Dem. Republic of Congo	-40
6	Indonesia	13,017	6	Brunei Darussalam	188	6	Malaysia	-35
7	Peru	8560	7	Marshall Islands	183	7	Cameroon	-30
8	Colombia	6805	8	Côte d'Ivoire	177	8	Tanzania	-24
9	China	6203	T9	Malta	173	9	Bolivia	-22
10	Bolivia	4442	T9	Martinique	173	10	Argentina	-17
11	Angola	4385	11	Malaysia	157	11	Myanmar	-16
12	Republic of Congo	3438	12	New Zealand	156	12	Peru	-15
13	Malaysia	3212	13	Republic of Congo	153	13	Papua New Guinea	-12
14	Suriname	3165	14	Slovenia	142	14	Colombia	-11
15	Argentina	3062	15	Jamaica	141	15	Zimbabwe	-10
16	Central African Republic	2861	16	Indonesia	138	T16	Angola	-9
17	India	2800	17	Kenya	137	T16	Mozambique	-9
18	Gabon	2710	T18	Cameroon	135	T20	Nicaragua	-8
19	Cameroon	2696	T18	Liberia	135	T20	Honduras	-8
20	Zambia	2416	20	Czech Republic	134	T20	Ghana	-8
				–	–	T20	Zambia	-8

information and thus the following information should be taken relatively lightly. Nevertheless, Table 5 gives an approximate idea of total carbon stocks and therefore suggests where future projects will be located.

When comparing the top 20 highest carbon stocks (either for a whole country or on a per hectare level) with the top 20 deforestation trends in 2000–2010 (i.e. net loss of hectares), the following countries are listed on both tables: Argentina, Bolivia, Brazil, Cameroon, the Democratic Republic of the Congo, Indonesia, and Zambia.

United Nations REDD Programme and the World Bank's Forest Carbon Partnership Facility

The two most prominent international institutions for REDD are the United Nations REDD Programme (UN-REDD Programme) and the World Bank's Forest Carbon Partnership Facility (FCPF).

The UN-REDD Programme essentially provides in-country technical assistance for the monitoring, reporting, and verification (MRV) of carbon emissions, along with assisting countries in the development of national REDD plans (i.e. REDD readiness plans).

As of November 2012, the countries with UN-REDD National Programmes are: Bolivia, Cambodia, Democratic Republic of the Congo (DRC), Ecuador, Indonesia, Nigeria, Panama, Papua New Guinea, Paraguay, the Philippines, Republic of Congo, Solomon Islands, Sri Lanka, Tanzania, Vietnam, and Zambia.

In addition, the other partner countries of the UN-REDD Programme as of November 2012 are: Argentina, Bangladesh, Benin, Bhutan, Cameroon, Central African Republic, Chile, Colombia, Costa Rica, Ethiopia, Gabon,

Ghana, Guatemala, Guyana, Honduras, Ivory Coast, Kenya, Lao PDR, Malaysia, Mexico, Mongolia, Morocco, Myanmar, Nepal, Pakistan, Peru, South Sudan, Sudan, Suriname, and Uganda.[66]

MAP 3. Partners of UN-REDD Programme[4]

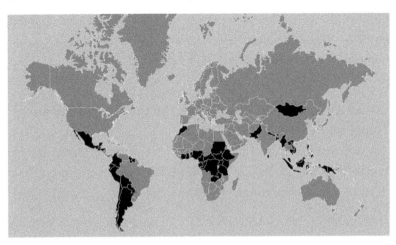

Similar to the UN-REDD Programme, the World Bank's Forest Carbon Partnership Facility includes the following, with many of the same countries (i.e. those bolded are members of both institutions) as well as some notable additions: **Argentina, Bolivia (Plurinational State of), Cameroon, Cambodia, Central African Republic, Chile, Colombia, Congo (Democratic Republic of), Congo (Republic of), Costa Rica,** El Salvador, **Ethiopia, Gabon, Ghana, Guatemala, Guyana, Honduras, Indonesia, Kenya, Lao (People's Democratic Republic),** Liberia, Madagascar, **Mexico,** Mozambique, **Nepal,** Nicaragua, **Panama, Papua New Guinea, Paraguay, Peru, Suriname, Tanzania,** Thailand, **Uganda,** Vanuatu, and **Vietnam.**[67]

MAP 4. Partners of World Bank's FCPF[4]

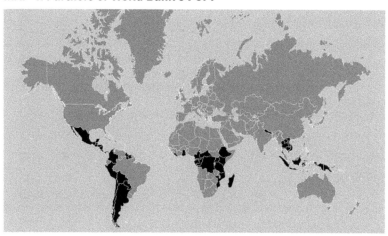

Similar to the UN-REDD Programme, the World Bank's Forest Carbon Partnership Facility:

Complements the UNFCCC negotiations on REDD+ by demonstrating how REDD+ can be applied at the country level and by learning lessons from this early implementation phase. The FCPF has created a framework and processes for REDD+ readiness, which helps countries get ready for future systems of financial incentives for REDD+. Using this framework, each participating country develops an understanding of what it means to become ready for REDD+, in particular by developing reference scenarios, adopting a REDD+ strategy, designing monitoring systems and setting up REDD+ national management arrangements, in ways that are inclusive of the key national stakeholders.[68]

Membership in either the UN-REDD Programme or the World Bank's Forest Carbon Partnership Facility demonstrates high-level country engagement with REDD+ initiatives which will facilitate the development of REDD+ projects and should mitigate some country-level risk.

Emerging financial innovations

Emerging financial innovations will enable a wider range of investors – such as institutional investors and high-net worth individuals – to participate in REDD+ projects and this will facilitate the scaling-up of REDD+ finance.

As previously mentioned, there are pooled funds being developed – such as the Althelia Ecosphere Fund – and the Terra Bella Fund has already engaged the Overseas Private Investment Corporation to provide political insurance for their project in Cambodia.

Other insurance products, such as protection against carbon stock reversals, could be developed in the future. Insurance products are important because they will enable investors to mitigate risk, while simultaneously enabling projects to be developed in countries with high rates of deforestation and high political risk.

The Climate Bonds Initiative is currently exploring ways to scale-up forest bonds which will be applicable to REDD+ projects.[69] There is also a chance for the US Agency for International Development (USAID) Development Credit Authority Product (DCA Product) to be adapted to forest carbon markets. This DCA Product currently underwrites loans, but is being adapted to underwrite bilateral agreements and provide a first-loss provision.[70]

Matt Leggett, head of policy at the Global Canopy Programme, explains:

One answer to a lack of interim demand for REDD+ credits could lie in concepts such as forward contracts. A forward contract for REDD+ (also known as an advance market commitment) would guarantee the purchase of REDD+ credits at a date in the future at a set price, and could create interim demand for credits in the absence of a globally binding agreement on REDD+ under the UNFCCC. This may represent a key avenue for private sector involvement in REDD+ between now and 2020, when it is projected that a global REDD+ mechanism may be rolled out.[71]

Thus, these emerging financial innovations have key roles the private sector can support to further develop the REDD+ sector.

CHAPTER 6
Concluding Remarks

FORWARD-THINKING SUSTAINABILITY LEADERS can help reverse tropical deforestation by engaging in payment for ecosystem service forest conservation projects, otherwise known as Reducing Emissions from Deforestation and Degradation (REDD+).

The synergy of supporting REDD+ activities and business sustainability includes, but is not limited to: mitigating global greenhouse gas emissions while reducing business risk to a changing climate; increasing consumer loyalty and improving businesses' connectivity to consumers while simultaneously benefitting upstream local communities and ecosystem services; enhancing corporate social responsibility image and upholding corporate principles; and providing marketing opportunities and product positioning through private sector support of REDD+ projects which can increase gross margins and net profits.

For businesses interested in supporting REDD+ projects, companies can: develop their own REDD+ project; donate to a nonprofit organization that is supporting REDD+ projects; invest in a company that is developing REDD+ projects; invest directly into a particular REDD+ project; or invest into a pooled fund.

Ultimately REDD+ provides a promising mechanism for financing forest conservation while increasing the sustainability and profitability of forward-thinking sustainable leaders; yet it is important to understand that time is of the essence as we are quickly losing tropical forests, the valuable ecosystem services they provide for free, along with jeopardizing the billions of livelihoods dependent on tropical forests around the world.

Further Reading

Center for International Forestry Research (CIFOR). 2012. *Analysing REDD+: Challenges and Choices* (Indonesia: CIFOR). Available at: **http://www.cifor.org/online-library/browse/view-publication/publication/3805.html**.

CINCS. 2012. *Engaging Private Sector Finance for REDD+*, 26 September (New York: CINCS). Available at: **http://www.cincs.com/media/upload/cincspublication/Forestracker_In_Focus_REDD_finance_FINAL.pdf**.

CIRAD. 2012. *Financing Options to Support REDD+ Activities*, April (Montpellier, France: CIRAD). Available at: **http://ur-bsef.cirad.fr/content/download/4123/32260/version/3/file/**.

Hall, Anthony. 2012. *Forests and Climate Change: The Social Dimensions of REDD in Latin America* (Cheltenham, UK: Edward Elgar Publishing).

Kissinger, Gabrielle, Herold, Martin and De Sy, Veronique. 2012. *Drivers of Deforestation and Forest Degradation: A Synthesis Report for REDD+ Policymakers*, August (Vancouver, BC, Canada: Lexeme Consulting). Available at: **http://www.decc.gov.uk/assets/decc/11/tackling-climate-change/international-climate-change/6316-drivers-deforestation-report.pdf**.

Oakes, Nick, Leggett, Matt, Cranford, Matthew and Vickers, Harry (eds). 2012. *The Little Forest Finance Book*, October (Oxford: Global Canopy Programme). Available at: **http://www.globalcanopy.org/materials/little-forest-finance-book**.

Related Resources

Carbon Finance. 2012. *About Us*. Available at: http://www.carbon-financeonline.com/company/about-us.html.

Environmental Finance. 2012. *About Us*. Available at: http://www.environmental-finance.com/about-us.

Governors' Climate and Forest Task Force. 2012. *About GCF*. Available at: http://www.gcftaskforce.org/about.

REDD Desk. 2012. *About the REDD Desk*. Available at: http://www.theredddesk.org/about_the_redd_desk.

Transparency International. 2011. *Global Corruption Report: Climate Change*, 2 June. (Washington, DC: Earthscan). Available at: http://files.transparency.org/content/download/103/415/file/2011_GCR climatechange_EN.pdf.

Transparency International. 2012. *Keeping REDD+ Clean: A Step-by-Step Guide to Preventing Corruption*, 26 October. Available at: http://www.transparency.org/whatwedo/pub/keeping_redd_clean.

United Nations Framework Convention on Climate Change. 2012. *REDD Web Platform*. Available: http://unfccc.int/methods_science/redd/items/4531.php.

Notes and References

ALL PHOTOGRAPHY CREDITS are due to Brian McFarland.

1. UN-REDD Programme. 2009. *About REDD*. Available at: http://www.un-redd.org/AboutREDD/tabid/582/language/en-US/Default.aspx.

2. Food and Agriculture Organization of the United Nations. 2011. *State of the World's Forests 2011, Annex, Table 2: Forest Area and Area Change* (Rome: FAO). Available at: http://www.fao.org/docrep/013/i2000e/i2000e05.pdf.

3. World Atlas. 2012. The List. Available at: http://www.worldatlas.com/geoquiz/thelist.htm.

4. Ammap. Date unknown. *Visited Countries Map*. Available at: http://www.ammap.com/visited_countries/index.php.

5. The Nature Conservancy. 2012. *Rainforests: Facts about Rainforests*. Available at: http://www.nature.org/ourinitiatives/urgentissues/rainforests/rainforests-facts.xml.

6. National Public Radio and Dr William Laurance. 2005. *Talk of the Nation: Amazon Rainforest Update*, 10 June. Available at: http://m.npr.org/story/4697219.

7. Organization for Economic Co-Operation and Development. 2012. *Members and Partners*. Available at: http://www.oecd.org/about/membersandpartners/.

8. Domask, J. 2004. International Development and Environment, Fall. Lectures at American University's Washington Semester Program.

9. Transparency International. 2012. *Corruption Perceptions Index 2011*. Available at: http://cpi.transparency.org/cpi2011/results/.

10. Brookings Institution and World Bank Group. 2012. *The Worldwide Governance*

Indicators (WGI) Project. Available at: http://info.worldbank.org/governance/wgi/index.asp.

11. Millennium Ecosystem Assessment. 2005. *Ecosystems and Human Well-Being: Synthesis* (Washington, DC: Island Press), p. V. Available at: http://www.maweb.org/documents/document.356.aspx.pdf.

12. Costanza, R., d'Arge, R., de Groot, R., Farberk, S., Grasso, M., Hannon, B., Limburg, K., Naeem, S., O'Neill, R.V., Paruelo, J., Raskin, R.G., Suttonkk, P. and van den Belt, M. 1997. *The Value of the World's Ecosystem Services and Natural Capital,* May. Available at: http://www.esd.ornl.gov/benefits_conference/nature_paper.pdf.

13. Pimentel, D., Harvey, C., Resosudarmo, P., Sinclair, K., Kurz, D., McNair, M., Crist, S., Shpritz, L., Fitton, L., Saffouri, R. and Blair, R. 2005. *Environmental and Economic Costs of Soil Erosion and Conservation Benefits,* February. Available at: http://www.rachel.org/files/document/Environmental_and_Economic_Costs_of_Soil_Erosi.pdf.

14. Steiner, A. and Dias, B. 2012. *The Biodiversity Bargain,* October. Available at: http://www.project-syndicate.org/commentary/from-deforestation-to-sustainability-by-achim-steiner-and-braulio-dias#MQGWOQCaExbkJPrr.99.

15. Costanza, R., Pérez-Maqueo, O., Luisa Martinez, M., Sutton, P., Anderson, S.J. and Mulder, K. 2008. *The Value of Coastal Wetlands for Hurricane Protection,* June. Available at: http://allenpress.com/pdf/AMBI-37-4-241.pdf.

16. Mendelsohn, R. and Balick, M.J. 1995. *The Value of Undiscovered Pharmaceuticals in Tropical Forests.* Available at: http://link.springer.com/content/pdf/10.1007%2FBF02862929.

17. Wilson, E.O. 2007. *The Creation: An Appeal to Save Life on Earth* (New York: W.W. Norton & Company, Inc.), p. 53.

18. Center for Responsible Travel. No date. *Responsible Travel: Global Trends & Statistics.* Available at: http://www.responsibletravel.org/news/Fact_sheets/Fact_Sheet_-_Global_Ecotourism.pdf.

19. Powers, W. 2006. *Whispering in the Giant's Ear* (New York: Bloomsbury USA), chapter 2.

20. Carbon Planet. 2009. *The History of REDD Policy*, 4 December, pp. 10–11. Available at: http://unfccc.int/files/methods_science/redd/application/pdf/ the_history_of_redd_carbon_planet.pdf.

21. Zwick, S. 2008. *Painting the Town REDD: Merrill Lynch Inks Massive Voluntary Carbon Deal*, 8 February (Washington, DC: Ecosystem Marketplace). Available at: http://www.ecosystemmarketplace.com/pages/dynamic/article.page. php?page_id=5584&section=home&eod=1.

22. Allianz. 2012. *Sustainability in Proprietary Investments: Carbon Investments*. Available at: https://www.allianz.com/en/responsibility/progress_report/ economic/proprietary_investments.html#.

23. Bank of America. 2010. Bank of America Merrill Lynch Supports The Nature Conservancy's Innovative Forest Project on Kalimantan, December. Available at: http://newsroom.bankofamerica.com/press-release/environment/bank-america-merrill-lynch-supports-nature-conservancys-innovative-forest.

24. Goldman Sachs. 2012. *Environmental Stewardship and Sustainability: Land Conservation*. Available at: http://www.goldmansachs.com/citizenship/ environmental-stewardship-and-sustainability/land-conservation/land-conservation-main-page.html.

25. Wheeland, M. 2012. *Puma's Eco-Impacts Report Kicks the Ball Forward on Transparency*, 10 February. Available at: http://www.greenbiz.com/blog/ 2012/02/10/pumas-eco-impacts-kicks-ball-forward-transparency.

26. Wildlife Works Carbon LLC. 2012. *Our Partnership with Puma*. Available at: http://www.wildlifeworks.com/press/puma.php. Wildlife Works Carbon LLC. 2012. *Our Carbon Neutral Supply Chain*. Available at: http://shop.wildlifeworks. com/pages/carbon-neutral-supply-change. Puma. 2012. *The Creative Factory*. Available at: http://www.pumalovethyplanet.com/.

27. EcoSecurities. 2010. Positive attitudes towards forest carbon offsets have

significantly increased in the past year, especially in Europe, May. Available at: http://www.climatestandards.org/news/files/Forest_Carbon_Offsetting_ PR_4_May_2010.doc.

28. Climate Markets & Investment Association. 2012. *Meet CMIA's Members.* Available at: http://www.cmia.net/WhoareCMIA/MeetCMIAsMembers/tabid/ 161/language/en-US/Default.aspx.

29. Code REDD. 2012. *About Code REDD.* Available at: http://www.coderedd.org/ about-code-redd/.

30. International Emissions Trading Association. 2012. *Our Members.* Available at: http://www.ieta.org/our-members.

31. Forest Carbon. 2012. *Forest Carbon Begins GIZ Funded Jurisdictional REDD Assessment in Laos,* 12 December. Available at: http://forest-carbon.org/ project-list/forest-carbon-begins-giz-funded-jurisdictional-redd-assessment-in- laos/.

32. Ministry of the Environment. 2012. Partnerships and Multilateral Initiatives. Available at: http://www.regjeringen.no/en/dep/md/Selected-topics/climate/ the-government-of-norways-international-/what-do-we-finance.html?id= 557700.

33. United States Agency for International Development's Forest Carbon, Markets and Communities (FCMC) Program. 2012. *US Government Investments and Policies to Facilitate Forest Carbon Finance and Markets,* March. Available at: http://www.fcmcglobal.org/documents/FCMC_USG%20Finance%20and%20 Markets%20Recommendations%20Final.pdf, pp. 19–20.

34. Chartered Financial Analyst Institute. 2012. *Code of Ethics & Standards of Professional Conduct.* Available at: http://www.cfainstitute.org/ethics/codes/ ethics/Pages/index.aspx.

35. Chartered Financial Analyst Institute. 2012. *Asset Manager Code of Professional Conduct.* Available at: http://www.cfainstitute.org/ethics/codes/ assetmanager/Pages/index.aspx.

36. Chartered Financial Analyst Institute. 2012. *Endowments Code of Conduct*. Available at: http://www.cfainstitute.org/ethics/codes/endowments/Pages/index.aspx.

37. Chartered Financial Analyst Institute. 2012. *GIPS Standards*. Available at: http://www.cfainstitute.org/ethics/codes/gipsstandards/Pages/index.aspx.

38. Overseas Private Investment Corporation. 2012. *What We Offer: FAQs*. Available at: http://www.opic.gov/what-we-offer/investment-funds/calls-for-proposals/global-engagement-faqs.

39. Yahoo. 2007. The Project Management Body of Knowledge (PMBOK), February. Available at: http://voices.yahoo.com/the-project-management-body-knowledge-pmbok-180818.html.

40. Olander, J. and Ebeling, J. 2011. *Building Forest Carbon Projects: Step-by-Step Overview and Guide*. Available at: http://www.forest-trends.org/documents/files/doc_2555.pdf.

41. Lawrence, S. 2010. *Climate Change: The U.S. Foundation Response*, February (New York: The Foundation Center). Available at: http://foundationcenter.org/gainknowledge/research/pdf/researchadvisory_climate.pdf.

42. PPR. 2012. *PPR Introduces Environmental and Social 5-year Targets across Luxury and Sport & Lifestyle Brands // PPR Acquires Stake in Wildlife Works Carbon, REDD Carbon Offsetting Company as Part of Next Phase of Sustainability Program*, 27 April. Available at: http://www.ppr.com/en/press/press-releases/ppr-introduces-environmental-and-social-5-year-targets-across-luxury-and-sport.

43. Nedbank. 2011. *Media Release: Nedbank Capital Helps Gucci, PUMA and Other Luxury Brands Achieve Carbon Neutrality*, 4 July. Available at: http://www.nedbank.co.za/website/content/corporate/capital_pr_detail.asp?section=press&subsection=Media%20Releases&article=current&prID=1262.

44. Volcovici, V. 2011. *Green Column: A Slow Start for the Carbon Credit Market*, 24 July (New York: New York Times). Available at: http://www.nytimes.com/

2011/07/25/business/energy-environment/a-slow-start-for-the-for-carbon-credit-market.html?pagewanted=all.

45. Environmental Finance. 26 July 2011. *Sustainable Forestry Deal of the Year.* Available: http://www.environmental-finance.com/features/view/595.

46. Ecosystem Restoration Associates Inc. 2012. *Carbon Projects.* Available at: http://www.eraecosystems.com/carbon_projects/.

47. Ecosystem Restoration Associates Inc. 2012. *Share Info.* Available at: http://www.eraecosystems.com/investors/share_info/.

48. Ecosystem Restoration Associates Carbon Offsets Ltd. 2010. *News Releases Forest Carbon Group AG Purchases 29.9% of ERA Carbon Offsets Ltd,* February. Available at: http://www.eraecosystems.com/investors/news_release/index. php?&content_id=105.

49. Ecosystem Restoration Associates Inc. 2012. *Company News: ERA Carbon Offsets Ltd Announces Acquisition of Offsetters Clean Technology Inc. and Carbon Credit Corporation,* 17 September. Available at: http://www.eraecosystems. com/whats_new/company_news/index.php?&content_id=184. Ecosystem Restoration Associates Inc. 2012. *News Releases: ERA Carbon Offsets Ltd Announces Signing of Definitive Agreements for the Acquisition of Offsetters Clean Technology and Carbon Credit Corp,* 8 November. Available at: http://www. eraecosystems.com/investors/news_release/index.php?&content_id=188.

50. CSR Wire. 2012. *ERA and Wildlife Works Deliver First REDD+ Project in the Congo Basin Rainforest,* 19 December. Available at: http://www.csrwire.com/ press_releases/35018-ERA-and-Wildlife-Works-Deliver-First-REDD-Project-in-the-Congo-Basin-Rainforest.

51. Marriott. 2012. *Why Preserve the Rainforest?* Available at: http://www. marriott.com/green-brazilian-rainforest.mi.

52. Kaplan, M.D.G. 2010. Marriott president: Why your sheets aren't washed nightly. *SmartPlanet.* April. Available at: http://www.smartplanet.com/blog/ pure-genius/marriott-president-why-your-sheets-arent-washed-nightly/3405.

53. Spain–US Chamber of Commerce. 2008. *News & Events: Other News: Merrill Lynch & Carbon Conservation Sign First Commercially Financed Avoided Deforestation Agreement*, April. Available at: http://www.spainuscc.org/newsevents/news-detail.asp?Language=English&newsID=182.

54. The Nature Conservancy. 2007. *Verification of Emissions Reductions from Avoided Deforestation: Noel Kempff Climate Action Project*, May. Available at: http://www.nature.org/ourinitiatives/habitats/forests/verification_of_emissions_reductions_from_avoided_deforestation_noel_kempf.pdf.

55. Environmental Finance Publications. 2011. *Terra Bella Carbon Fund.* Available at: http://www.environmental-finance.com/download.php?files/pdf/4d67868d72b39/carbon%20funds11_sample2.pdf.

56. Terra Global Capital. 2011. *Terra Global Secures Investment Capital for REDD and Land-Use Carbon Fund*, 3 November. Available at: http://www.terraglobalcapital.com/press/Terra%20Global%20Capital%20Secures%20Investment%20Capital%20for%20REDD%20and%20Land%20Use%20Carbon%20Fund%20Press%20Release%20Nov.%203%202011.pdf.

57. The Forest Carbon Partnership Facility. 2012. *Introduction.* Available at: http://www.forestcarbonpartnership.org/fcp/node/12.

58. Carbon Finance Unit at the World Bank. 2012. *BioCarbon Fund.* Available at: http://wbcarbonfinance.org/Router.cfm?Page=BioCF&ItemID=9708&FID=9708. Carbon Finance Unit at the World Bank. 2012. *Introduction.* Available at: http://wbcarbonfinance.org/Router.cfm?Page=BioCF&FID=9708&ItemID=9708&ft=About.

59. International Finance Corporation. 2012. *BioCarbon: Summary of Proposed Investment.* Available at: http://www.ifc.org/ifcext/spiwebsite1.nsf/ProjectDisplay/SPI_DP28977.

60. Kett, H. 2011. *Macquarie and Partners Build $25 Million Partnership to Find REDD Projects*, 31 August (Washington, DC: Ecosystem Marketplace). Available at: http://www.ecosystemmarketplace.com/pages/dynamic/article.page.php?page_id=8516.

61. Althelia Ecosphere Fund. 2011. *Althelia Ecosphere Initiates Ground Breaking Public-Private Partnership for the Development of Forest Carbon*, 9 November. Available at: http://www.ecospherecapital.com/wp-content/uploads/2011/11/AltheliaEcosphere_PR_09Nov11_Final1.pdf.

62. Conservation International. 2011. *Conservation International Enters into Groundbreaking Partnership with Althelia Climate Fund on REDD+ Investments*, 9 November. Available at: http://www.conservation.org/newsroom/press releases/Pages/Conservation-International-Enters-into-Ground-breaking-Partnership.aspx.

63. European Investment Bank. 2012. *Althelia Climate Fund*. Available at: http://www.jaspers.europa.eu/projects/pipeline/2010/20100720.htm.

64. The State of Acre, the State of Chiapas, and the State of California. 2010. *Memorandum of Understanding on Environmental Cooperation between the State of Acre of the Federative Republic of Brazil, the State of Chiapas of the United Mexican States, and the State of California of the United States of America*, 16 November. Available at: http://www.gcftaskforce.org/documents/MOU_Acre_California_and_Chiapas.pdf.

65. Food and Agriculture Organization of the United Nations. 2011. *State of the World's Forests 2011, Annex, Table 3: Carbon Stock and Stock Change in Living Forest Biomass* (Rome: FAO). Available at: http://www.fao.org/docrep/013/i2000e/i2000e05.pdf.

66. UN-REDD Programme. 2009. *UN-REDD Programme Partner Countries*. Available at: http://www.un-redd.org/Partner_Countries/tabid/102663/Default.aspx.

67. World Bank's Forest Carbon Partnership Facility. 2012. *REDD+ Country Participants*. Available at: http://www.forestcarbonpartnership.org/fcp/node/203.

68. World Bank's Forest Carbon Partnership Facility. 2012. *About the FCPF*. Available at: http://www.forestcarbonpartnership.org/fcp/node/12.

69. Climate Bonds Initiative. 2011. *Forest Bonds*. Available at: http://climatebonds.net/resources/our-publications/unlocking-forest-bonds-5-messages/.

70. Durschinger, L. 2012. *The California Carbon Market and the Role of International Forests: A Primer on the Risks and Opportunities for Institutional Investors*, 6 November.

71. Leggett, M. 2012. *Another False Summit for REDD+ at Doha?*, November. Available at: http://www.carbon-financeonline.com/content/analysis/another-false-summit-for-redd-at-doha.html (subscription required).

....

For Product Safety Concerns and Information please contact our EU
representative GPSR@taylorandfrancis.com
Taylor & Francis Verlag GmbH, Kaufingerstraße 24, 80331 München, Germany